No Longer Water

A Chapbook of Poetry
Katrina Kaye

ECHOBIRD
PRESS

Address inquiries in permission to:
Echobird Press, echobirdpress.com
ISBN 981-1-961370-00-5 | ISBN 981-1-961370-01-2 EPUB

Contents

Re Shape

I disentangle myself
        from the woman
I used to be

        allow her
                to rest

her time   well spent
has ended

        and now

I mold with broken fingers
        and roughened palms

another cast
another face

        eyes and bones
                and stitched lips

I do not recognize
in the mirror

        only to shed her
        in time as well

and begin
            again

Dreams

I dismantled my dreams,
boxed them, stacked
my closet shelves.

They grow dusty beside
shoes and short skirts
I don't wear as often
as I thought I would.

For years these dreams waited,
only to be unwrapped upon occasion
tried on, just to see if they still fit.
But they are not for keeping.

I am done.

I've come to that cold,
melancholy realization
that I will never have
the guts to remove the tags.

Instead, I rewrap them,
bestow them, make peace
as I give them to you
one by one.

I do not intend them
as a curse, although
I can attest to the lack

of joy they have brought
time after time. I hope
they will do more for you
than they ever did for me.

I hope they will fit
and you can twirl merrily
to each new step.

These things:
dreams, hopes, love,
the intangible aspects
of myself I wanted
so badly to create,
to keep and harvest,

they are not meant to be.
I know that now.

I release them to another,
no regrets, no goodbyes.

Balance

i am
dove

and
tightrope
walker

balancing
act

don't let
me fall

this
time

just wait
just
wait

soon
enough
there will
be harmony

let me
mourn

bend
and
break

let my
heart
scab over
and heal

i will
find
my footing

i will
make
it
across

Everyone has a Summer

Mine involved boys and alcohol,
late nights, loud music and bonfires,
a little red dress I bought on sale.

I balanced on platform shoes,
etched black eyeliner around lashes,
eager to be a little more than what I was.

I used to smoke cigarettes.
It was an excuse to make
eye contact, slip away with someone,

discuss poetry — or was it
philosophy? — share a strawberry flavored
kiss, and whisper a secret or two.

There was a summer I danced
on a block at the Pulse nightclub
to Siouxsie and the Banshees

almost every Thursday night
in that little red dress with the open back
and side slit, neon light and billowing smoke.

Everyone has a summer,
but there is no reason to be dismayed
when the fall comes.

Even in autumn months,
a night or two may recapture me
to a place of little consequence.

There are still late nights
when I have a drink too many,
kiss the boys on the patio,

kiss the girls on the neck.
Smoke a cigarette from
the brand I quit years ago.

I watch myself in mirrors shadowed
with soot, see my city lie in dust,
and wonder who else feels the chill in the air.

I've grown past the green of my prime,
and, although I wane, there is a young woman
with a too loud laugh wearing a red dress

who still exists somewhere in the pit of me,
because giving in to the animal
until the sun rises can be so breathtaking.

Disinfect

perhaps
the only way to heal
is to open the wound

water is not
always enough
sometimes fire
is needed

let the sting
of disinfectant
sizzle and smart until
toxicity subsides

extinguish the bacteria
that spreads and
breeds in darkness
with water and fire
and antiseptic burn

promises of reform are
not driving cells to rebuild

hopes and prayers
and well wishes
do not flush a wound
they merely dismiss it
leave it coarse

allow the infection
to spread
until it becomes
                intolerable
untreatable
                consuming
        permanent

the wound is necessary
        for growth to begin
the wound is necessary
        to awaken the body

do not be afraid
of the scar that remains
it is proof of survival
                of healing
of resilience
        it is proof repair is possible

the scar defines identity and
gifts a narrative
unique to its terrain

the scar is a blessing

Three Days

allow body
release from
the weight
of the last
few months

insides crave
to be carved
free from that
which binds

feel skin
loosen
bone peek
through what
dares remain

tonight
the sunset
serves witness
to this request

not for rebirth
not for pledging anew
but as a break
to the pattern

three days
is all that is needed
to take the
thickness of torso
grounding of muscle
and shake loose

allow healing
        even if not complete
        even if only to prepare
        for the next wound

break unconscious acts
let body refresh

like creek
water on
sunny morning

like the sound
of screen door
slapping shut

Mirror

the mirror is warped
it flatters me to the right
and ripples me to the left
an unreliable narrator
telling the story of
the person I have become

my eyes are not consistent
they change color in the light
they shift an image
from a cloud to a carousel
they focus on the detail
and miss the larger picture

how long have I been
mistaking self portraits for landscapes
seeing the line where the shore ends and not the sea

but isn't there a beauty in a pinch of sand
that the dunes in all their glory cannot match
a world that cannot be seen without microscope
and closer examination

it is easy to become lost in the minutiae
despite the hope of the horizon

In Between

the woman I was is desperate
to find conciliation with
the woman I will be

we come together inside aging skin
and seek a stretch of days
to cradle what cannot be forfeit

I am not yet finished

I create the new
out of fragments of what was

there is an innocence
exchanged for the seasoned

the trivial mixed with the essential
and all the slippery spots
in between

seeking a union, a compromise,
a complete version ready to embrace
all that is to come

Voice

My speech
shudders
inside me,

a tornado
siren,

a wail
in my gut,

the echoes
fade fast.

Where did my voice go?

There was a time
I could go on,
each word scorching
the tongue of
the last.

Now
I find my voice subdued.

Now
I find
I skirt the floor
with the debris of curse
words.

I no longer
spiral pronunciations
around tongue
but let sound
idle.

Voice
needs room
to grow,
a space
to share.

Voice
needs to
cling to the
octaves of
rib cage
and swing

and scream
and hold tight,
and not be surprised
when the waves buck us
from our feet.

Unfinished

there is a trench
dug against my navel

running between breasts
concaving into clavicle

a ravine
through the center of me

this is where
I need to be filled

it doesn't matter
if it is love that floods the chasm

or pebbles of hope piled
one upon the other

it doesn't matter if it is a spell
to resurrect the dead

or songs which conjure oceans
and summon the mountains

it could be the sweetness of sunrise
kaleidoscoping before my eyes

displayed against bare ceiling
while last's night coda repeats in my head

it could be anything that is pure
simple and peaceful

it only needs to complete me
fill me, make me whole

but these fleeting sentiments
have yet to fill the hollow

for now, I remain gutted
with little hope of being finished

Mule

I am mule.
My bay, an obnoxious yap
from graying muzzle
as I move from
under a master's whip.
My velvet ears twitch
with distrust for the acts of man.

I will not be owned
and have grown impatient
with the repeated acts of
those who claim to know what's best,

so I become obstinate,
with mud to my knees,
rebelling by standing still,
immovable in open stall
despite the whistle on the wind.

I want only a gentle hand but deny
those offered me as though
their compassion was insult or pity.

No longer do I hold desire to plough forward,
but I long to preserve the moments
as they are gifted, one sunset, one thoughtful word,
one cube of sugar, one kindness at a time.

Hopefully, this perseverance
will lead me to dry pastures where only
the occasional fly distracts from
solitude and peace.

Kate Once Told Me

every poem begins
as a suicide note.

And a
well rehearsed
death
is always
winkled inside mind,

soaking there,
dripping stalagmites,
building blocks of
the subconscious.

Counting ticks
to midnight;
the story
so close
to conclusion.

Loneliness,

like rock candy
crystallizing on
popsicle sticks,
attaches to rib cage,

expands and compresses
with each
shallow breath.

I do not have fear.

Sometimes the
only thing
that gets me through
is knowing

at any minute
I can stop it all.

I can rock and roll
out of this human suit,
shed soft covering,

reveal bare bone,
and empty cavern.
The sliver of power
over my life;

it is everything and
it is nothing.

Father

Allow a streak of light
from single bulb hallway
to lay across the floor.

Remind me, in this mild action,
there are heroes in the world,
not every action is based on
the selfish hunger of men.

On nights like this
the rocks of the world
lay heavy on my spine,
pinning me to an earth
I have no desire to inherit.

It is why I am well versed in
the tongue of loneliness.
I am most concrete
wrapped in solitude.

Let me hear the voices
down the hall. The influx
in cadence regardless of meaning,
the occasional laugh.

I am again
five years old asleep in
a stranger's house feeling
no desire to resume the
party but comforted to know
it continues.

Leave the door cracked,
just enough, so I'll know
when the house rings silent,
when the hall light finally dims
that I am completely alone.

Turning Tricks

I am not the girl I was before,
but not all these tricks are new.

Some remain trapped inside
pulled muscles and survival instinct.

Disfigurement of fingerprint bruises
on fourteen year old trachea.

White striped scars against tanned skin.
Tiny circles of cigarette tips

left on the underside of American thighs.
Old tricks concealed in the green casing of jade scarves,

ill patterned tattoos and skirts cut at the knees.
There is a metamorphosis scratching,

a change of perception hanging upside down
from the higher branches. Discoloration solidifies,

a healing of harm inflicted on adolescent flesh.
Balancing acts shift from high beam to fingertips.

Sleeves conceal tricks of trade
instead of slices at the nape of wrist.

I am not the girl I was before
but not all these tricks are old.

A reformation recognizable not only
in breast bone and high forehead,

but in the pacing of breath
and the stillness of soul.

Cocoon continues to cling to branch.
Skin sheds over five life times,

caterpillar remnants catch on ankle,
but they do not hold you back,

Transform under the thumb of time,
crack chrysalis into a thousand sharp flecks

puzzle the pigments into a newly formed pattern,
still crumpled and wet with the residue of rebirth.

Disappear

I am
      disappearing act,

mispronounced
name,   forgotten
      introduction.

I walk with cat feet,
      and sew lips
      to keep breath hushed.

I am as unsubstantial
      as the chill
that comes with the dark.

Part ghost,
part chameleon.

I wish
I could
      say there was
         security in
the anonymity,

but it merely
leaves me
      hollow and creates
a blotch
      only I can see.

Don't try
        to look
for me.

I blend
        into background,

then disappear
        as quickly
as a song

which you never
        bothered
to remember.

Lullaby

the past plays wind instruments
outside bedroom window
a lullaby from a childhood
that slipped by too fast

it's a tune that has gone unheard
for decades, yet I seem to know
the arrangement of notes
and can anticipate the changing pitch

it is not the numbed silence
that comes from the stillness of strings
and quietude of auditorium we want
but to hear the continuance of the melody
there is no rush to get to the end

the present does not play melody
but sounds like static
from the television
left on across the room
the hum carries consistency

how can we hear the past
when the present is a distracting buzz
when the future is blaring its inevitability
so loud it rattles the windows

the bedroom leaks a ray of light
from east facing window
illuminating the dust that sways through stale air

this song isn't urgent to finish
but to be heard
as it crests and crescendos

No Longer Water

I no longer swing from storm to puddle
or flood the basement during freak winter storms.

I no longer cleanse the dirt from hands and face,
nor do I provide blessing or baptism.

I have become as inconsequential
as sea splatter drying on rocks.

I used to hold ships afloat on my back,
and I'm sure I drowned a man or two in my youth

back when I was all hips and hurricane,
back when I was unruly ocean,

but my tumultuous surf has proven tedious
and the seascape too vast for waning current.

I no longer erode mountain or stone.
I no longer flow around obstacles or caress hands.

And no longer do the seasons affect my consistency.
I no longer freeze in the winter, nor do I fall in April.

I no longer offer nourishment or encourage creation.
I am no longer necessary.

I am no longer needed,
I am extra, gratuitous.

I am no longer water and yet I remain
bound to this tangible earth for a little longer.

Perhaps I have become the wind,
not essential air but lazy breeze

that does little more than cool
a swimmer fresh from the sea

or carry a leaf from branch through
the ether to its final resting place.

I am not strong enough to break a branch,
nor angry enough to shake the house or creek the walls.

I do not howl; I whisper,
barely strong enough to scatter seeds.

And Now I

steal a moment
under the clutter of
ceiling fan loose
at its screws
and the breeze
from open window
advertising a night
more temperate
than the day
more quiet and
peaceful than the
rumble of mind

I have chosen to settle

I loved nights
like this when I was younger
when I spent little
time indoors and allowed
myself the freedom
and recklessness
I thought was the
promise of life
I am glad I lived it then

nights like this

making out in a car
with the first boy I
fell in love with

walking with blissful
intoxication
through a city street

driving under the stars
just outside the city limits
where the light finally rests

dancing in the dark
as I walked downtown
with someone I barely
knew but trusted completely

I wish I remembered more

I wish I hadn't spent
so much time looking
toward the next moment
and enjoyed the one in which I swam

I didn't take it all for granted

how many times
have I had the privilege of
lying with eyes puddled closed
feeling content with what
I have lived
believing there was nothing more
life could gift me

it continues its kindness

and although I am sometimes
clouded with doubt, I too
recognize the love
the ability
the beauty
the full gift of life

I am not one to use the word 'blessed'
and the word 'luck' trivializes the sensation

I am gifted in this life and despite pain,
disappointment, failure, and setback
I have so much

I fill with gratitude
with feelings of having more
than I deserve
what more can I ask
what more is there to attain

these words are a two headed serpent
and cannot translate the race of language or
the fullness of thought clouding my mind

I will not use this moment
to make any grand resolutions
but I will allow the freedom
of heart and mind to find my peace

I am grateful for this moment
with sleeping dog at my side and
mewing cat on the shoulder of couch
the loud crank of the ceiling fan
the breeze of the night through open window
it does not tempt me to places I have once been

It merely reminds me
of the glories of a life
I am grateful to have lived

Release

I practice release:

For too many years I kept
carcasses baited on hook,
held skeletons long
after their slow decay.

My house reeks of
decomposition.
The dust piled heavy
on unread books,
the sand on windowsill
that comes from the
March winds.

It is time to practice release:

Open windows,
leave doors ajar,
allow the cat to slip in
and out around unkempt stoop.

Burn poems, pictures, throw away
artwork piled behind dressers.
Dismiss the bundled burden of
birthday cards from shoebox.

All the keepsakes that define
who I was are no longer relevant
to whom I have become.

Let them dissolve into sand
and seep through fingers,
sticking and scattering
where it may.

Be Content

with sunlight
through kitchen window

the recorded
sounds of violins and
wine from a stemless glass
with a smudge
of lipstick on the rim

be not disappointed
with each souvenir
you have wrought

in an attempt to surrender
seclude to kitchen table
ask the weight on
shoulders to retire

take pen to paper if desired
enjoy a glass of red wine
and much needed solitude
let the music
move from neckline
to fingertips

as it always has
as it always will
understand every gift
at your fingertips
is hard earned
and the loneliness

that too

has been invited

Begin Again

begin with the ocean

the wet sand
hard underfoot

the waves seeping in
soft foam sticking
to ankles as
the water pulls us

soak in an
overcast day in
northern california

shirts untucked

gulls coasting
high above on a
salty chill

arms around chest
to secure warmth

notice toes
curling and uncurling
embedding small flakes of
broken down life
in the crevasses
between nail and skin

we can begin by observing this
small moment of time
as though it were everything
because at this moment
it is everything

we can begin by allowing
the wind to pull us forward
instead of letting the earth
hold us back

Acknowledgements

The author would like to gratefully acknowledge the following publications for previously publishing a version of the following poems:

"Dreams" is previously published in *You Might Need to Hear This* (2021).

"Disinfect" is previously published in *Door is a Jar* (2023).

"In Between" is previously published in *Introspection Quarterly* (2022).

"Father" is previously published in *Chariot Press* (2022). *Talon* (2022), and *Greatest City Diary* (2022)

"Disappear" is previously published in *Mollyhouse* (2022).

"No Longer Water" is previously published in *Verse Virtual* (2023).

"Be Content" is previously published in *The Green Shoe Sanctuary* (2022).

"Unfinished," "Mule," Everyone Has a Summer," "And Now I," "Voice," "Kate once told me," "Three Days," are previously published in *Saturday's Sirens* (2021-2023).

About the Author

Katrina Kaye is an educator, writer, publisher, artist, and community organizer.

A lifelong creator, she has been published in various ezines, magazines, and anthologies. She also spent time on the performance stage, touring across the United States and participating in various poetry festivals and events, before hanging up her microphone in 2015.

She is the author of two chapbook collections, two out of print collections, and three current books through Swimming with Elephants Publications, LLC. She is currently anthologizing her collected works on her website entitled: Iron & Sulfur: The Abandoned Writings of Katrina Kaye (poetkatrinakaye.com).

Katrina lives gratefully and happily in New Mexico with the love of her life. She continues to write, occasionally perform, and publish her own writing.

Other Poetry by Echobird Press

The Gatekeeper Wears Acrylics by Court Winterborne
the bones of this land by Kat Heatherington
A Map Without Your Shadow by Kat Heatherington
(coming Winter 2024)

Fiction by Echobird Press
www.echobirdpress.com

Friends With Wings by Maxwell Pearl
The Alters series by Terra Katherine McKeown